# My Amazing Body
# MOVING

Angela Royston

Raintree
Chicago, Illinois

Editorial: Marta Segal Block, Catherine Clarke,
Nick Hunter, Jennifer Mattson
Design: Roslyn Broder, Kim Saar
Illustrations: Will Hobbs
Picture Research: Maria Joannou, Pete Morris
Production: Sal d'Amico, Jonathan Smith
Printed and bound in China by
  South China Printing Company.

08 07 06 05 04
10 9 8 7 6 5 4 3 2 1

**Library of Congress Cataloging-in-Publication Data:**
Royston, Angela.
  Moving / Angela Royston.
    v. cm. -- (My amazing body)
Includes bibliographical references and index.
Contents: Inside and out -- Taking shape -- Making
bones move --
Throwing and lifting -- Gripping and holding --
Walking and running --
Jumping and hopping -- Bending and twisting --
Nodding and shaking your
head -- Talking and smiling -- What can go wrong --
Exercising your
muscles and joints -- The whole body.
  ISBN 1-4109-0482-2 (lib. bdg.)
  1-4109-0951-4 (paperback)
 1.  Human locomotion--Juvenile literature. [1. Human
locomotion. 2.
Body, Human.]  I. Title. II. Series.
  QP301.R696 2004
  612.7'6--dc21
                          2003006444

**Acknowledgments**
The publishers would like to thank the following for
permission to reproduce photographs:
pp. 4, 12, 14, 18, 22 Pete Morris; p. 5 Science Photo
Library (Alfred Pasieka); p. 6 Science Photo Library
(Prof. P. Motta/Department of Anatomy, University "La
Sapeinza", Rome); p. 7 NHPA (Ernie Janes); p. 8 Corbis
(Tom and Dee Ann McCarthy); p. 11, 16, 19 Science
Photo Library (D. Roberts); p. 13 Science Photo Library
(CNRI); p. 15 FLPA (Minden Pictures); p. 17 EMPICS
(Tony Marshall); pp. 20, 23, 27 Corbis (Ariel Skelley); p.
21 FLPA (Foto Natura Stock); pp. 24, 26 Corbis (Bob
Rowan, Progressive Image); p. 25 Science Photo Library
(ZEPHYR); p. 28 EMPICS (Phil Walter).

Cover image of a thermograph of the human body
reproduced with permission of Corbis (Howard
Sochurek). Small photograph of children exercising
reproduced with permission of Corbis (Roy Morsch).

The publishers would like to thank Carol Ballard for
her assistance in the preparation of this book.

Every effort has been made to contact copyright
holders of any material reproduced in this book. Any
omissions will be rectified in subsequent printings if
notice is given to the publishers.

The paper used to print this book comes from
sustainable resources.

# Contents

Any words appearing in bold, **like this,** are explained in the Glossary.

# Inside and Out

Whatever you do, it usually involves moving part or all of your body. You move your legs when you walk, jump, and run. You bend your arm and move your hand when you lift up a book or open a door. Your back and head also move.

You can move your arms, legs, head, and other parts of your body into many different positions.

## Inside your body

You can see what happens on the outside of your body as you move your arms and legs, but you cannot see what is happening inside. You can move only because you have **bones** and **muscles** inside your body. Your muscles make your bones move. As your bones move, the rest of your body moves, too.

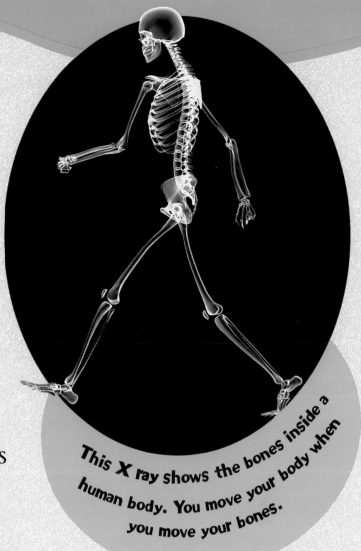

This X ray shows the bones inside a human body. You move your body when you move your bones.

## How animals move

Animals can move around, too. Animals look different from people, partly because their bones are different shapes and sizes. Animals move differently from us, too. Cats and many other animals walk on four legs. Although animals look very different on the outside, they have muscles and bones inside, and their bodies work in a similar way to our bodies.

# Taking Shape

You cannot see your own bones, but you can feel them. When you feel your body, you can feel soft **flesh** below your skin. Under the soft flesh is hard bone. Babies are born with more than 250 bones, but some of these slowly join together. By the time you are an adult you will have about 208 bones. Together they make up your **skeleton**.

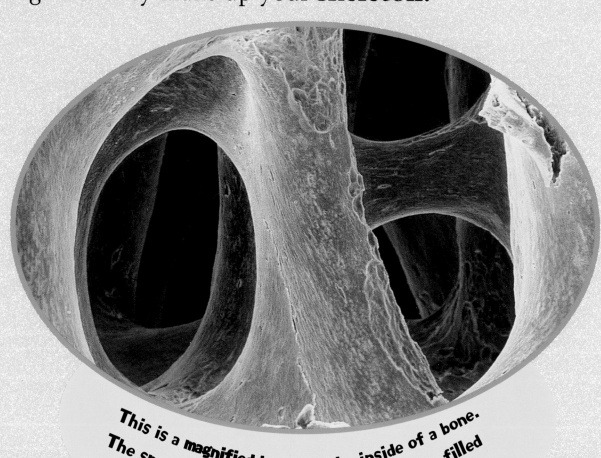

This is a magnified image of the inside of a bone. The spaces in a bone are actually tiny and are filled with air, which makes the bone lighter.

## A strong frame

Your skeleton is a frame that gives your body its shape. Your **limbs** (arms and legs) are long and straight because the bones in them are long and straight. The bones in your back keep your back straight. Without bones you would flop like a rag doll.

## Protective shield

Some bones protect important parts of your body. Your **ribs** protect your heart and **lungs**. Your **skull** protects your brain inside your head.

## Animal skeletons

Many animals have bones like ours, but their skeletons are not the same shape. A dog and a human both have a head, **spine** and four limbs. People and dogs can both lie on their stomachs, but a dog cannot always take the same position as a human.

A dog lies down in a different way from a human because its bones are different shapes.

# Making Bones Move

**Muscles** are part of the soft **flesh** you can feel over your **bones.** A muscle is attached to the bone it moves by a strong band of **tendon.** When you clench the muscle it becomes shorter and tighter. The tendon then pulls the bone to make it move.

This man has large muscles in his upper arms. He is using them to hold the block above his head.

## Bending your foot

Most of the muscles that move your feet are in your calves, the soft flesh behind your shin. Feel your calf as you lift your foot and point your toes. You should feel the muscles becoming tight and hard.

shoulder joint

tendon

biceps muscle

triceps muscle

tendon

elbow joint

You use the muscles in your upper arm to bend and straighten your lower arm.

## Bending and straightening your arm

Muscles work by pulling on a bone. They cannot push. This means that you use a different muscle to straighten your arm than to bend it. The muscle in the front of your upper arm is called the biceps. You use this muscle to bend your arm. To straighten it again, you have to relax your biceps and tighten your triceps. The triceps is a smaller muscle on the back of your upper arm.

## Chest muscles

You use muscles in your chest to lift your whole arm. Orangutans have large, strong chest and shoulder muscles. They use them to swing and lift their long, powerful arms.

# Bending and Twisting

When you bend down to pick something up, you have to bend your back. Your back is made up of many small, knobby **bones** called vertebrae. The way they fit together allows you to bend forward, backward, and to each side. The vertebrae also allow you to twist around to look over your shoulder.

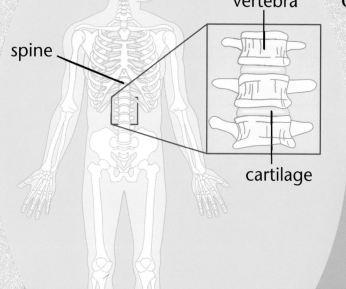

spine

vertebra

cartilage

## Your spine

You have 33 bones in your back. They make a long column called your **spine.** Your spine is very strong. It holds your head up, and many other bones, such as your **ribs,** are joined to it.

*Because of the way the vertebrae in your spine fit together, you can move your body into many different positions.*

## Moving your spine

Many things you do involve moving your spine. Movements such as walking or throwing a ball would be very difficult if your spine was **rigid** like a pole. When you are sitting or standing, muscles in your back work together to keep your spine upright.

You can see from this colored X ray how snakes bend their long backs into coils. This corn snake's spine is shown in purple.

## Amazing spines!

A snake has more than 150 bones in its spine! It has no legs, so it wriggles and bends its spine to push itself forward.

# Throwing and Lifting

When you throw a ball or lift something heavy, you use your arms in different ways. When you throw a ball you swing your arm at the shoulder. When you lift something, you bend your elbows and lift your lower arms. Your shoulder and elbow are both **joints.** The way the **bones** fit together in a joint controls how the bones can move.

When you throw a ball underhanded, you swing your arm at the shoulder.

## Swinging your arm

You can move your arm at your shoulder in almost any direction you want. The reason for this is that your shoulder joint is a ball-and-socket joint. The top end of your upper arm bone is round, like a ball. It fits into a round cup in the shoulder joint. This lets your upper arm swivel (move) in all directions.

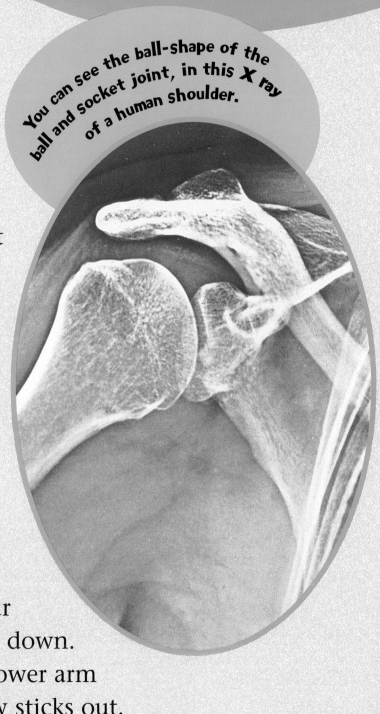

You can see the ball-shape of the ball and socket joint, in this X ray of a human shoulder.

## Bending your arm

Unlike your shoulder, your elbow only moves up and down. You can only bend your lower arm toward you, so your elbow sticks out. Your elbow is called a hinge joint because it moves like the hinge on a door that opens and closes.

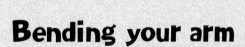

# Gripping and Holding

When you write, you hold the pen or pencil and make many small movements. At the same time you move your hand across the page.

Writing is one of the most difficult things you do with your hands and fingers.

## Gripping a pen

When you hold a pen or pencil, you grasp it between your fingers and your thumb. You can only bend and straighten your fingers, but your thumb is joined to the rest of your hand in a special **joint.** This joint allows you to move your thumb around and touch each of your fingers on the same hand.

## Moving your fingers

The **muscles** that move your thumb and fingers are all in your lower arm. These muscles are joined to your finger bones by long **tendons.** If you bend and straighten your fingers, you can feel the tendons moving in the back of your hand.

Birds can bend their claws around a perch but they cannot grip and use a pen the way you do.

# Walking and Running

Walking, running, skating, and dancing are some different ways of moving that use your legs. You also move your legs when you kneel or sit down. You use different **muscles** and **joints** to move your legs in different ways.

Your knee is a hinge joint. It lets you swing your lower leg backward and forward. The kneecap bone protects your knee.

## Walking

Although walking is one of the easiest ways of moving around, it uses over 200 muscles! Each leg has many different sets of muscles. Muscles in your back and arms help to keep you balanced.

Sprinters run very fast over a short distance. A sprinter uses her arms and her legs to give her the power to run fast.

## Running

When you run, you lift your legs higher and move them faster than when you walk. As you take each stride, you bend and straighten your legs at your knees. Each knee is a hinge joint but your hip is a ball-and-socket joint. This means that your leg can move backward and forward, and also in a circle at your hip.

## Animal sprinters

Horses, cheetahs, ostriches, and many other animals can run much faster than people. They have long legs and strong muscles to help them run so fast.

# Jumping and Hopping

Hopping and jumping are more difficult than walking and running. They are more difficult because you have both feet off the ground at the same time.

## Jumping

When you jump, you first bend your knees. Then you push your feet against the ground to push your body into the air. Running before you jump helps you to jump higher and farther.

These children are playing hopscotch. They are using their muscles to hop from square to square and to keep their balance.

## Hopping

Hopping is like jumping, except that you jump on one leg. Hopping is harder to do than jumping because you have to balance on one leg as well as move around.

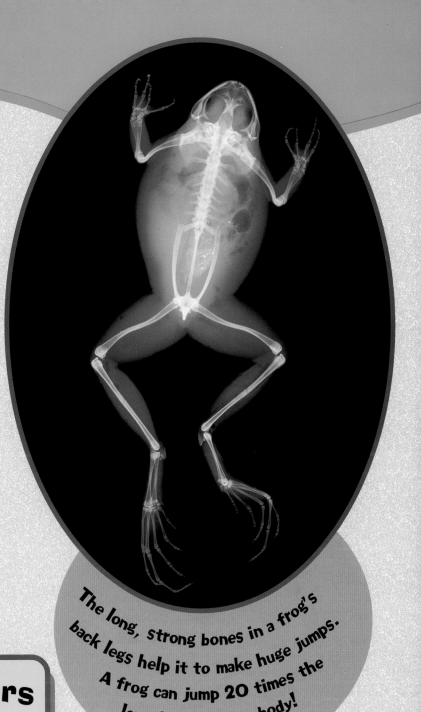

The long, strong bones in a frog's back legs help it to make huge jumps. A frog can jump 20 times the length of its own body!

## Champion jumpers

Some animals are very good at jumping. Frogs and kangaroos neither walk nor run. Instead they leap using their long back legs. When they jump, they bend their back legs and push themselves into the air.

# Nodding Your Head

You can move your head up and down and around. **Joints** at the top of your **spine** allow your head to move in all these different directions.

## Moving your head

You have two joints in your neck that allow you to move your head in different ways. One joint lets you move your head from side to side. Another joint lets you tilt your head up and down. Together these two joints let you move your head to see all around you— behind your back, down to your feet, and up in the sky.

The joints in your neck let you move your head to look in different directions.

A cat cleans itself by licking its fur. It can move its neck and head to reach almost every part of its body.

## Holding your head up

The thick bone you can feel when you touch the top of your head, is called your skull. It protects your brain, and is very heavy. **Muscles** in your neck work hard to hold your head up. If you relax those muscles your head immediately falls forward.

# Eating, Talking, and Smiling

Apart from the **muscles** that move your lower **jaw,** most of the muscles in your face do not move **bones.** Instead they move the **flesh** that makes up your cheeks and lips, and covers the other parts of your face. These muscles work together when you talk, laugh, and frown.

## Eating and talking

When you eat, you open and shut your mouth and move your cheeks and tongue to push the food around your mouth and down your throat. When you talk you use muscles to move your lips, tongue, and mouth into different shapes to form different sounds.

The muscles that open and shut your mouth are in your cheeks and are some of the strongest muscles in your body.

## Smiling and frowning

The flesh that covers your face is not very thick but it is packed with muscles. You use about fifteen different muscles when you smile. These muscles stretch your lips and pull up the corners of your mouth. When you frown, muscles in your forehead pull your eyebrows together, while other muscles make your mouth turn down.

### Faces show feelings

Humans, more than any other animal, use their faces to show how they feel. When you smile, you are probably happy or pleased. When you frown, you may be angry or puzzled.

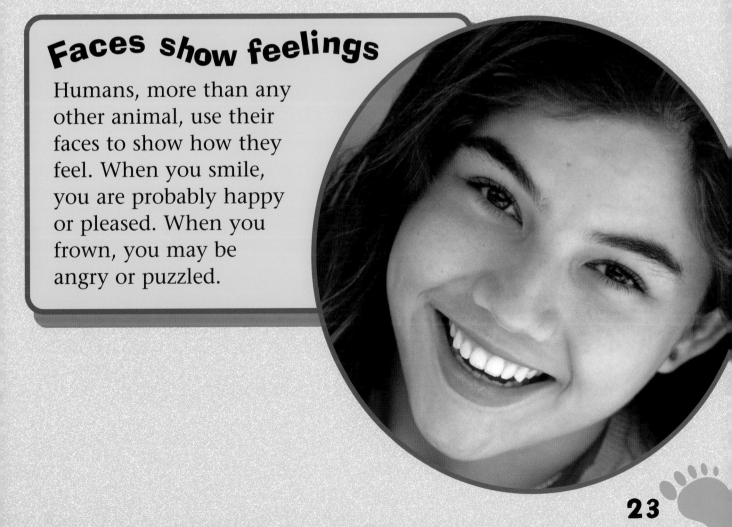

# What Can Go Wrong?

Your **bones** and **muscles** work well to keep your body moving, but sometimes things go wrong. If you fall awkwardly, you can hurt a **joint,** bone, or muscle.

## Spraining a joint

When you sprain a joint, you overstretch the **ligaments** that hold the joint together. A sprained joint hurts, particularly when you try to move it. You need to rest the joint until it is better.

A bandage helps to support a sprained joint while it heals.

24

## Breaking a bone

If you break a bone you have to go to a hospital where the bone will be **X-rayed.** The X-ray shows where and how much the bone is damaged. If you break a bone in your leg or arm, a doctor will probably wrap it in a **cast.** The cast protects the injured bone while it heals.

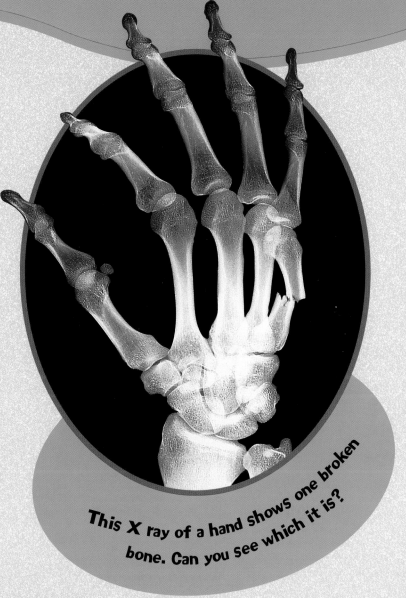

This X ray of a hand shows one broken bone. Can you see which it is?

## Pulled muscles

If you stretch a joint too far, you may pull one of the muscles or tendons that are connected to the joint. A pulled muscle hurts when you move it.

# Exercising Your Muscles and Joints

Exercising your **muscles** and **joints** keeps them strong and healthy. Walking, running, and helping with jobs around the house are all good ways of exercising your muscles. Swimming, dancing, and playing on a climbing frame also exercise your joints.

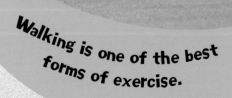

Walking is one of the best forms of exercise.

## Strong muscles and joints

The more you use your muscles, the stronger they become. If you sit around all day, your muscles will become weak and flabby. Your heart is a muscle, too, so exercise makes it work better. Exercise stretches the **ligaments** around your joints. This allows you to move the joint further without injuring it.

## Keeping your balance

It is difficult to stand on one leg for a long time. Muscles all over your body have to work hard to stop you from falling over. Learning to dance, rollerskate, or ride a bicycle will help you to improve your sense of balance.

Dancing moves your joints, exercises your muscles, and improves your sense of balance.

# The Whole Body

When you move your body, you use more than your **muscles, bones,** and **joints.** Your whole body has to work together. Your heart and **lungs** work harder so that you can keep moving. Your eyes and ears tell you what is happening as you move, and your brain controls how you move.

This tennis player watches the ball carefully. Her brain controls how she moves her arms and legs to hit the ball.

## Heart and lungs

Your heart pumps blood to every part of your body, including your muscles. The blood contains **digested** food, and **oxygen** from the air that you breathe in. Muscles use up sugar and oxygen as they work. The harder your muscles work, the more food and oxygen they need. This makes you breathe more heavily and causes your heart to beat faster.

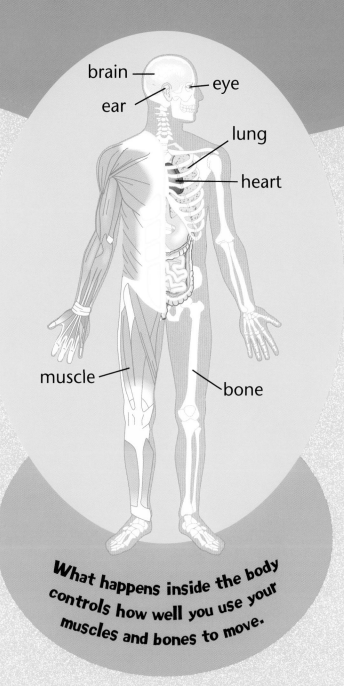

brain
eye
ear
lung
heart
muscle
bone

What happens inside the body controls how well you use your muscles and bones to move.

## Controlling your muscles

Your brain controls your whole body, including your muscles. Your eyes, ears, and sense of touch tell your brain what is happening. When you decide what to do, your brain sends messages to your muscles to make your body move.

# Find Out for Yourself

Everybody's body is slightly different but they all work in the same way. Find out more about how your own amazing body works by noticing what happens to it. Can you feel which muscle is tightening when you move a part of your body? Can you touch your toes without bending your knees? How many different bones can you feel in your hand? You will find the answers to many of your questions in this book, but you can also use other books and the Internet.

## Books to read
Royston, Angela. *Why do Bones Break? And Other Questions About Bones and Muscles*. Chicago: Heinemann Library, 2003.

Royston, Angela. *Broken Bones*. Chicago: Heinemann, 2004.

## Using the Internet
Explore the Internet to find out more about moving. Websites can change, so if some of the links below no longer work, don't worry. Use a search engine, such as www.yahooligans.com or www.internet4kids.com, and type in keywords such as "bones," "muscles," and "exercise."

## Websites
www.kidshealth.org contains lots of information about how your body works and how to stay healthy.

www.brainpop.com. Click on "Health" for quizzes and films about different parts of the body, including bone structure and broken bones.

# Glossary

**bone** hard part of your body below your skin and flesh

**cartilage** rubbery substance at the ends of bones that stops them from grinding against each other

**cast** hard covering that surrounds a broken bone to protect it while it heals

**digest** break up food inside the body

**flesh** soft parts of the body between the bones and the skin

**jaw** bone in the head that holds the upper or lower teeth

**joint** place where two or more bones meet and fit together

**ligament** band of strong flesh that covers the outside of a joint and holds the joint together

**limb** legs and arms

**lungs** parts of the body where oxygen from the air passes into the blood and carbon dioxide leaves the blood before being breathed out

**magnified** made to look much larger than the actual size

**muscles** parts of the body that you use to move

**oxygen** gas that all living things need to survive

**rib** one of the long, thin bones in your chest that protect your heart and lungs

**rigid** stiff and not bendy

**skeleton** all of the bones in your body

**skull** thick bone that protects your brain and other parts of your head

**spine** your backbone. It is made up of 33 smaller bones.

**tendon** strong cord that joins a muscle to a bone

**X ray** kind of photograph that shows parts of the inside of your body, such as your bones

# Index